The Thoughts and Emotions of a King

By

Marlon E. King Jr.

Proem

Throughout my life I have experienced a lot. Most of my experiences were first hand experiences of things I went through. While some of my other experiences were a result of something that I witnessed. I bring this up because everything that I have experienced, all the good and bad, has made me into who I am today. Which has led me to writing this book, which in a way is a reflection of myself. Specifically, a reflection of my feelings and thoughts relating to the things which I have experienced. As with many experiences in life, some of the poems that you will read in this book will be good, some will be bad, some will arouse you, some you will relate to, and some you will not. While I haven't enjoyed every experience that has led to me writing this book, I have enjoyed writing everything that is in this book, and I hope you enjoy it too.

With thanks,

Marlon E. King Jr.

Despite everything that I have ever written, there is not poem, a paper, or a story that will ever mean more to me than my first poem. I wrote it when I was sixteen and have been writing poetry ever since. And so, I feel it only right that your first experience with my poems be with my first experience writing poetry.

ill fated

The Little boy so proud,

the little boy so happy,

the little boy told a secret to those who shouldn't have known.

Now the little boy's parents are gone and he is left all alone.

Not his fault, but I guess he was just born *ill fated.*

The little boy now not so little

is bullied and pushed around wherever he goes.

Not his fault, but I guess he was just born *ill fated*

Now the little boy is nearly a man,

loves a girl who doesn't love him.

His heart burns with the knowledge

that she will never love him the same way

that he loves and cares for her.

Not his fault, but I guess he was just born *ill fated*

Now the boy is a fully grown man,

unsatisfied and disgusted with his life.

He goes to the drawer and draws a knife

then proceeds to write

a goodbye letter to all those he's ever met in his life.

As he finishes his last sentence

he pulls the knife across his throat and whispers "goodbye"

to the life that he wishes he had never known.

It was not the little boys fault

For he did not ask for the life he was given

But I guess like many others

he was just born

ill fated.

My Lady

The woman from around the way,

the one I see but never speak to.

Her presence controls me

and leaves me speechless whenever she's around.

Her smile warms my being and brightens my day,

yet the fact that she never notices me

makes me feel insignificant and non-existent.

And still, I treasure and hold dear

all the times that she comes near me.

This beauty whose name I do not yet know.

She is simply she,

my lady,

my love,

the woman I wish to know.

Incomplete thoughts

To me

she is beauty

full

of life, emotion, and

happiness

is what she brings to me.

Obsessed

I can't sleep

probably because I'm not really tired.

The medication I was prescribed

has long since stopped working.

I really don't want to be awake,

because all I've been able to do as of late

is think of her.

The woman I want, but can't have.

Her name is Sabrina,

she's a waitress at a local cocktail bar

and a full time student at a local university.

She is also by far

the most beautiful woman I've ever seen.

She stands at about five nine

and weighs round about

one hundred and sixty-three pounds.

Her natural wavy dark brown hair flows down to the small of her
back

and her almond shaped eyes

are an amazing shade of hazel green.

She smells like a sweet combination

of fresh cinnamon rolls

and a Hawaiian breeze glade plug in.

Her smile always seems to lift me up

and give me reason to continue living.

From her window I can see

the layout of her well kept

one-bedroom apartment.

You would think

that she was an interior designer

based off the kind of class and taste

her home furnishings displays.

However, her taste in men

is overdue for some reevaluating.

For the guy that she is currently dating

doesn't deserve her by any means.

For starters, he's a mechanic at a subpar car shop

and he's only just now started

taking classes at a nearby community college.

Hardly the kind of person

deserving to have the title

of being Sabrina's man.

My mother thinks that

me and Sabrina are dating

based off the way I constantly talk about her.

If only I could be so lucky,

but unfortunately no such luck.

My psychiatrist on the other hand

thinks that I'm obsessed with her.

Personally, I find that to be impossible

I mean after all,

I've only been stalking her for eleven months.

Allure

Like when night comes over day

She creeps over me and into another place I go…

Addiction

This pain within me

hurts me so much

that I cannot think clearly.

Why is it that I feel this pain?

This deep hurt that no one sees

but I feel so strongly inside.

Much like that of a mother

whose child has died unexpectedly in infancy.

Continuing to live with this pain

is something that I do not feel

I can do much longer.

And so I give myself freely

to those who would desire me

so that I can obtain the substance I need

to dull out my pain.

My hands and body shake

and cold chills run through me

as sweat drenches me and my pain worsens.

I spark a flame to this drug which I've obtained

so that I may fill this used syringe I've found.

My eyes have become wide

as I look upon my salvation

with anticipation

of the relief that it will soon give to me.

My heart is now racing with excitement

like that of a giddy child

waiting to receive his gifts on Christmas.

So I take the tip of this dull syringe

and force it into my skin.

I wince at first,

but then I smile

for as I push down

my relief begins.

Relief that comes as rush,

much like the first time having an orgasm

in a long time and falling in love

all at once.

Now my pain,

my shaking,

and my cold sweats have stopped.

My body relaxes now and my breathing slows

and as this happens

my eyes become heavier and heavier

to the point that they close.

So now I drift off to sleep

hoping that when I wake

I will feel as good as I do now.

However, it doesn't really matter though.

For if the pain does come back

and I do start to shake and sweat again,

I just gotta do what I gotta do

to get another hit

so I can get this feeling back.

Failed Escape

I nearly died last night,

though it wasn't for

a lack of trying on my part.

I had taken a variety of medicinal pills

and locked myself in the bathroom

hoping that my pill cocktail

would put an end to things soon.

Had some aspirins for the headaches,

a number of sleeping pills for the insomnia,

and all of my anti-depressants

because life itself can no longer make me smile.

Soon after,

my mind starts to become fuzzy

or I might have been dizzy,

hard to recall the difference.

Then my body becomes real heavy

which is weird

cause I felt like I was floating.

I know my breathing began

to slow down a lot.

Before I knew it,

nausea set in

and I started to vomit.

From what it looked like,

I think it was the

meatballs and spaghetti

that I had for breakfast.

I had read somewhere

that you shouldn't try and kill yourself

on an empty stomach.

However, what was meatballs and spaghetti

now looks like thickened gravy

and curdled milk

with the smell to match.

I fall face first into it,

and don't mind it at all.

My pill mix seems to have

made me rather cold,

and so the warmth of my vomit

actually feels pretty good.

I hear something,

is that someone knocking on the door?

Or is that banging?

I can't really tell the difference

and I don't really care to know.

I blackout,

or am I sleep?

Maybe this is what death feels like,

who knows.

All I know is that

for the first time

since my father

and his many friends

showed and told me

the many ways they loved me

I'm at peace.

That is,

if sticking their tongues

into my ear and kissing on me

is a way of talking.

And if by having

their hands hugging my waist

as they penetrated my ass

and left me covered

in their sweat and semen

as way of showing they love me.

All while keeping me locked in a basement

and repeating their ways

of displaying affection,

sometimes doing far more,

from the time I was six

until I was sixteen years old.

There's light ahead,

is that heaven?

No, it looks familiar,

kind of like a

bright neon light.

I'm feeling light headed and woozy.

This can't be right,

I shouldn't be feeling anything.

Wait, what's that beeping sound?

Is that a heart monitor?

I'm, I'm in a hospital.

But how did I get here?

And why am I alive?

Ah man,

the banging on the door

that I heard earlier.

Mike must have

came home early and saw my note.

Guess he called 911,

just my luck

that I would get the paramedics

who are actually good at their job.

Great,

now I'm stuck here.

Tube in my throat

and strapped to this fucking hospital bed.

Why is it

that I can't seem to escape

this hell that I call life?

Sounds like the door is opening

Oh goody,

It's my savior Mike.

And, who is that with him?

No!

Anyone except you

Anyone except

My father.

As I lay here crying and helpless

he walks over and rubs his hand

across my face.

Kisses me on forehead

smiles and tells me,

"don't worry son,

everything is going to be okay".

Why?

why couldn't I just

escape…

Fearless

I'm not afraid of needles,

I think it's a trait

that I get it from my mother

because of how well acquainted

she was with them.

I don't fear violence,

probably because of the ways in which

I was beaten by my father

for no other reason

than the fact that I was there.

I don't fear death,

mainly because I welcome it.

If I were being honest,

I don't fear anything.

Had you lived

the life that I have

I doubt you'd fear anything too.

Moment of Clarity

From being ill fated
to being exalted and free.

From moments of sadness and despair
to other times filled with blissful glee.

Many have tried to hurt me
but none have been able to keep me down.

Though many times I have faltered
I have always risen up stronger

This may seem to be nothing more
than ranting or boasting to you.

But I stand strong in believing
that this is my moment of clarity.

What a Place

What a place.

What a place we live in today.

A place that so many see as great

because of all the things that are given,

never realizing what is kept

from the deserving

or taken away.

What a place.

What a place.

Where men can hate a boy

simply because of the color of his face

and the supposed sound

which parted from his lips.

The men's hate festers

and turns into rage,

a rage that causes them to take the boy away

from the family which the boy stays.

To then beat the boy and taunt him.

Slash the boy and choke him.

Until the young boy's heart gives way.

And his mutilated body

is not discovered

for several days.

While all know that

it was the hateful men

who killed the young boy,

only a few seem to care.

So the hateful men go on about their lives unmoved

or remorseful of what they have done.

Yes. Yes. Yes.

What a place.

Such a great place we live in indeed.

Where things like this are done.

What a place we live in.

What a place.

What a place indeed.

Nightmare

Last night

I dreamt that I was being robbed.

Even after the thief got what he wanted

he shot me three times.

I fell forward, unable to move,

and laid there in a pool of my own blood.

As I tried to breathe

I felt like I was drowning.

I thought about trying to swim,

but I don't know how.

Besides,

I was feeling too numb to move

so I closed my eyes and relaxed.

I never woke up

from that dream.

Then again,

maybe I wasn't dreaming...

Endless Possibilities

I wake up

the same as always,

nothing out of the norm.

I wipe the crust out of my pie shaped eyes,

walk into my bathroom

and stare into the mirror.

As I look at myself,

I see nothing.

Which makes me feel empty.

Much like the empty vodka bottles

that are scattered across

my bedroom floor.

However,

me and those vodka bottles

greatly differ in comparison.

For even when empty,

a vodka bottle is worth something,

or can at least be useful.

So I pick up a knife

and press it to my neck.

Preparing myself

to cut into the core of my apple.

But as I continue to look at my reflection

in the mirror,

I smile.

I put the knife down,

then I turn and walk away.

I think that today will be a good day.

Conflicted

We met recently,

though I wish we had met

years before.

For in the short time

that we've known each other

you've grown on me immensely.

Our conversations

flow with ease

and bring about

an exceptional level

of happiness within me.

I frequently find myself wondering

how things would be

if we could work to be

something more than

what we are now.

Physically,

I find you to be flawless.

Personally,

I've come to see you

as being unique

in more ways than one.

The intimate moment we shared

has since caused my feelings for you to deepen

and has also caused me to want you

in a different way than I had before.

You deserve more than

what you receive.

And I want nothing more

than to be the one

who relieves you

of all of your pain and stressors.

But I can't be who you need

because I'm still working on

improving me,

and figuring out where I want to be

as well as who I want

to be beside me.

I can only hope

that we can one day be

more than what we are now.

The Three L's

She came on my face.

It felt like warm syrup

because of how

smooth, thick, and wet it was.

Although, it didn't taste like syrup.

Rather, it tasted more like

a strawberry and pineapple

jam mix.

The fact that her womanhood

was odorless

made it all the better.

Needless to say,

I liked it.

She took me to her

family's house

not long after that.

With the way they treated me,

you would think that

I had already met them,

I could tell they liked me a lot.

Later that night,

she told me

that she loved me.

I kinda felt bad

about the fact

that I didn't say it back.

We broke up

about a week ago.

When she asked me why,

I told her that I used to like her

and that I thought

one day I could love her.

But in all actuality

I only lusted her.

S.M.I.L.E for me (She Made It Little Easier)

She tells me to smile

but for the life of me

I don't know why.

For the way things seem right now

I have nothing to smile about.

I received a final write up at work,

I got an eviction notice yesterday,

and my mom relapsed last week

and no one's seen or heard from her since.

So why on Earth should I smile?

And why does she want me to smile?

For the life of me I don't know.

But as I look at her now

I can't help but want to smile.

And then I realize

that she's given me a reason to smile.

Because as I look at her

it feels as though

my problems and concerns

don't bother me much anymore.

As I look at her

I see someone

I'd like to work alongside

to build something with.

And it doesn't matter the type of relationship

because I know with her

anything created would be positive.

When she speaks to me

and I see her smile

I find peace

which reminds me

of when I was a child

and life was much simpler

than what it is now.

In our conversations,

she tells me about

how she loves

and cares for her children so much,

which leaves me a little envious

because I myself

never knew the joys of

a mother's support and love

in the way in which she shows it.

But the energy she gives off

leads me to believe that

her love is something special.

Unfortunately,

I feel that neither of us

are in a place

where we can currently be

an anchor and tether for the other.

But I can say

with a smile on my face

that her actions,

her words,

and the smile on her face

has made it easier for me

to make it through another day.

Thank me later

I stroked you.

Slowly at first,

no sense in starting fast

and ending early.

Plus, I find the experience

to be more pleasurable

when time is taken to fully enjoy the act.

Once I caught a comfortable rhythm

I began stroking you faster.

The sensation was exhilarating

and my heart fluttered as I brushed my fingers

across the curves of your full shape.

The marks that I'm leaving on you

will be sure to have other women

jealous with envy.

As well as teach anyone

who views you

about how passionate I was

while putting work into you.

At last,

with my final stroke

I came

to an end

of the face portrait I drew for you.

I truly hope you like.

You can find a way

to thank me later

if you do.

Guilty Pleasure

So uh,

about me

putting my dick

in your mouth?!?

I mean,

it doesn't have to be

my *whole* dick.

I was thinking

just as long as it's enough

to graze the back of your throat

and cause you to gag a little.

If it's any consolation,

you can ride my face

while you do it.

Being that tomorrow

is your birthday

which makes you a cancer,

doing sixty-nine

only seems right.

Plus, I figured

that I could bless you

with the gift of spectacular dick,

while helping myself

to eating some of that cake

that you got.

From the taste test

that I got from

my fingers,

I must give my compliments

to the chef.

Clearly you been

eating plenty of

pineapple and honey

based off how sweet you're tasting.

Rather than you

experiencing your deliciousness

from tasting your fingers

or mines.

I think it would be best

if I were to use the

head of my penis

to gather up

some of your sweet secretion

and have you experience

one lick at a time.

I have no desire

for you to experience

the full flavor

of what's inside

my king size tootsie pop

just yet.

Instead I'll bend you over

and continue to eat you,

because my beard

isn't soaked with enough

of you yet.

After about an hour or so,

you're begging me

to stop what I'm doing

because now your lips are swollen

and your clit is throbbing

from me showing

them so much attention.

So I relieve you

of my mouth,

but now my dick

is about to cause you some problems.

Being that your ass is still moist

from me having ate it,

I slowly slide the head

of my dick

and full length of my shaft

into it.

I can't tell if

your moaning

and screaming out

in pleasure or pain

as you claw into the sheets.

And truthfully

I don't care,

for it all sounds like

music to my ears

to me.

After spending a while

fucking your backside,

I lay you on your back

and place your feet near my shoulders

so I can fuck

a different area of your insides.

I'm sucking on your toes,

squeezing your nipples,

and biting on your calves

all while stroking

in and out of you.

Your pussy is so good

I went from saying,

"Damn, I love it" to

"Damn, I love you".

I pull out

cause your shit

is just too amazing

and I was starting to get

that *I'm about to cum feeling*.

Then,

like some shit out of the exorcist,

you turn and start to give me head

upside down.

Got me like,

"this chick done went from

earning herself a free movie and meal

to earning herself a spa day

and a trip out of town".

Your technique is flawless.

You rotate from fondling my balls

and taking in all of my dick

into your throat

to stroking it with your hands

while massages my balls

with your mouth.

You feel my legs

start to shake

as I'm beginning to cum,

and just like

the disgusting freak you are,

you let me shoot my seed

into your mouth and onto your face.

Smiling and still licking

my softening dick the whole time.

Which leads me to believe

that you must like the way

it feels and how it tastes.

I lay down

as you get up

to clean yourself off

and get yourself together.

It's really unfortunate

that I got a girl

cause after that performance

you really got me wishing

that we could be

together.

Null and void

Over the years

it's often been said

long hair,

short hair,

no hair,

don't care.

Well me personally,

I got standards

and certain shit that I expect

from a woman I'm going to be

fucking with.

So with that said,

I need for everything below a woman's eyebrows

to be completely bare

and void of hair.

Because the only hair

that should be on a woman's face,

aside from the hair above her eyes,

should be my pubic hair.

From when the head of my dick is in her throat,

or slapping against her forehead,

or sliding down against her nose,

or moving across her cheeks and eyes as she sucks my balls.

Now,

baby girl

you've told me that you want to try new things

and being the freak that I am

I'm all for it.

So I thought I'd start by

putting my thumb

wrist deep in your ass

while I'm fucking you from behind

ought to help me show it.

You scream and shout

mine and Jehovah's name.

So I grab you by the back of your neck

and shove your face into the pillow

cause I'm not trying to hear your mouth later

about how you got another fucking noise complaint.

I ease up,

then pull out of you slowly

to take a break from fucking you,

which causes you to get nice and quiet.

Then I proceed to

spread your cheeks apart

and slowly lick up your thighs

while biting on your ass,

until finally sticking my tongue inside it.

After some time eating your ass

I'm still quite hungry,

so I turn my attention to your soaking wet pussy

in the hopes that eating it will fulfill me.

After spending some time

eating you out,

I turn you over

so that you're lying on your back

with your legs spread apart

and your ankles resting on my shoulders.

I then begin my assault on your swollen wet pussy.

I start off with long slow strokes,

which I enjoy so much

due to the fact

that I can feel your pussy kegeling

each time the tip of my dick and your g-spot touch.

Next I begin to fuck you

with quick short thrusts,

switching between the two styles

so as to ensure that you continuously cum.

As I'm fucking you

you're scratching my back up

which I'm sure will leave scars,

luckily for you baby girl

I don't mind at all.

Cause I find pleasure

in pain,

which you'll learn more about

next time around.

Ffffuuuuccccckkkk

your pussy is so fucking good

and I'm starting to get the feeling

that I'm about to cum soon.

I'm fucking you raw

so I pull out of you as I'm cuming

soiling both your skin and your sheets,

cause I be damn if I get caught up

with my kids in your stomach

unless you're just digesting them.

As good as that was baby girl

our time is over now,

so I wash myself up

and hand you a few

 much needed wet wipes.

Then quickly get dressed and leave

without giving you a kiss,

saying goodbye,

or goodnight.

Because kissing is something intimate

and cuddling is for lovers and friends

and all that shit

is null and void

when we're just occasionally

fucking each other.

Ms. Loose

What am I going to do?

Why now?

Why me?

With everything going on right now

a baby is the last thing I need.

I mean,

I got school,

my job,

my friends,

plus things I want to do

with my life.

Not to mention

I'll have to hear shit

from my worrisome ass family.

Momma always be tripp'n as it is.

And my little brothers

Reggie and Tyrell always be in my business.

They'll just think that shit is funny

and end up telling everybody once they hear about it.

The saddest part is,

I don't know who the father is.

I'm three weeks late right now,

and if I think back on it,

I was with Kyle that Friday

but then I was with

John the Sunday

of that same weekend.

And even though me and Kyle

been together for about

seven months' now

and he treat me right,

he don't be there like that

like I want him to be.

I mean I get he tryna do what he need to do

to be good with school and his team

so that he can get into college,

but I still got needs too.

I mean,

I doubt that John's the father anyway.

I mean I only let him hit me raw

that one time.

Any other time

I make sure

he uses a condom.

It's not like anyone knows

I'm messing with John.

But what if it is his?

Do I tell Kyle?

John wouldn't care,

I mean we not together.

And he'll probably

just tell me I ain't his girl

so it ain't his problem.

Plus,

he already got two

other kids

with someone else

so I doubt he want me

carrying his third.

And with Kyle tryna go to college

I doubt he'd want to deal with

having a baby anyway.

But then again,

Kyle a good dude

so I'm sure he'd stay around

if it was his.

Wait!

I got it.

I'll just stop messing with John,

then I'll have sex with Kyle again.

I'll wait a week or so

and tell him that I'm pregnant

and that it's his baby.

He'll have no reason

to not believe me.

That way

he can still go to college

and get rich

from either playing ball

or getting a good job.

That way

he can take care of me and the baby,

or he can stay here

and take care of me and the baby.

Either way me and my baby will be taken care of.

And even if he decides

that he can't deal

and he wants to leave,

I still got

my family and friends

that can help take care of

me and the baby.

That's what my momma did

when she had me

and my daddy left,

and look how I turned out.

So often,

I find

that my thoughts

take me places

that my emotions

refuse to

let me leave…

Trapped Queen

Her physical shape

is nothing short

of utterly amazing.

As her curves bend in every right direction

which causes swarms of

would be suitors

to approach her

from every direction.

She has a smile

that can soften a harden heart

Sadly,

her state of mind

is in a state of distress

and in need of

intensive reconstruction.

For she has been

misguided by society,

and the men in her life,

whom have led her to believe

that she's a bad bitch

whose sum worth

is determined by

the number of

likes, labels,

and money she receives.

However,

I see her potential

at the heart of her soul.

And because of what I see

as being possible with her,

I love her so.

So patiently I wait,

pray, and hope

that my trapped Queen

will realize her worth

and find her way.

So that she may take her place

beside I,

her King,

so that we may fulfill

our great destinies

that lie before us

as King and Queen.

Unity

I am alone.

You are alone.

If we were alone together,

then we'd no longer be alone.

Pleasure

The stubble against my face

feels like the prickly ends of a hair brush.

I slide my fingers into the center of her yoni,

anticipation building within us both

as I do so.

The warmth which her garden exudes

has my hand sweating

and my mind racing

about what it is

that I should do next.

I look down at her

in awe as her body flows up and down

like the waves of an ocean

in response to my lingham

now stroking in and out of her.

As I place my mouth on her areola,

I bite it gently to increase

her level of stimulation.

She inhales deeply and begins to shake

as she has reached her climax.

Then she becomes quiet and still

like the calm

after the storm has passed.

We embrace one another

and drift off into a pleasurable sleep.

Thoughts

Yes,

I am staring at you.

And yes,

I am thinking of some exceptionally

inappropriate and freaked out things

pertaining to me and you.

You're looking more curious than offended

so I'll take that as you want to know

what thought has crossed my mind

pertaining me and you.

Well, if I were being honest,

several thoughts have crossed my mind.

All of which I'm more than willing to tell you

if you really want to know.

One thought in particular

that crossed my mind

was to have you suck my balls

while I fuck your titties

till I cum on your face.

Then have you

lick the nut off your lips

while telling me

how much you

love how I taste.

However,

if gargling balls

and getting facials isn't your thing,

another thought I had

was to have you

face down and ass up

at an angle like Gumby's dome.

And stroke life out of you

until it's time

for the early morning cartoons

to come on.

Don't worry boo,

my thoughts aren't all about

doing what will please me.

Cause after we leave here tonight,

I thought we could skip

Waffle House and Ihop

and head straight to my house

so I could get you to hop

your ass and pussy onto my face

and get yourself some of this

good mouth

and let me find out

how you taste.

But enough about me

and my thoughts.

I'm trying to find out

what you thought about

in regard to what I had to say.

Cause I'm hoping

that the thought has crossed your mind

for us to act

my thoughts out sooner,

rather than later.

Wondering

So *uuuhhhh…*

I was wondering,

if I were to

french kiss

the lips between your hips

for the next hour or two,

while occasionally giving your clit

delicate eskimo kisses

as a means to

set the mood,

would you mind

letting me

fuck you from behind

with this rather impressive

stroke that I've perfected

that's sure to improve

the curvature of your spine?

I know,

I am talking a bit reckless.

But I mean look at you,

physically you're amazing.

So of course

I can't help but to want

to be intimately involved

with you.

Even now,

as I look at you,

the shape of your mouth

and the curvature of

your hips, ass, and breast

got me lusting you badly.

So much so

that I was wondering

if I could stroke

the inside of your throat

till I cum

and have you

throwing up my kids

onto your neck and chest

while my balls rest

on your face?

Huh?!?

Oh,

well they'd be resting there

because of the upside down position

that I would have you in.

I find it's the best position

for receiving fellatio

just in case your husband comes home early

and I need to leave out

without being seen.

And yes,

I did notice your wedding ring.

But since I don't see

your husband around

I figured I'd see

if the wedding ring

actually means anything.

I *kknnnooowww*

I'm rambling and talking crazy,

but it actually brings me

to something that I

had wanted to say to you

but had forgot to.

See, I once heard

someone say that

too much pressure busts pipes.

So I was wondering

if you wouldn't mind

pressing the full weight

of your ass

against my pipe

so I can enter you

and bust off in your colon

before the end of the night?

I know,

I know,

I know.

You're probably thinking

that I'm an ol nasty,

rude, and disrespectful ass

muthafucka right?!?

While that may very well be true,

it's beside the point.

Cause this ol nasty,

rude, and disrespectful ass

muthafucka was wondering,

can I do

everything that I talked about

with you?

Can I?

Good evening,

I don't mean to be too forward

but I happened to notice

that your left ring finger

was looking a little light

and free of restraints.

So I was wondering,

if you don't have any plans

for later tonight,

can I take you back to my place

to test out your willingness to use restraints

and see how much pleasure and pain

you can take?

What's that?

Oh, I apologize,

you're right.

It seems my curiosity

and lust for you

has caused me to lose

my manners tonight.

My full name is

Dis Negah Nasti.

And yes,

you heard me right.

You can call me

any variation of my name

as long as you make sure

you say it with respect

when you do.

So you can call me Dis,

Dis Negah,

Dis Negah Nasti,

or Mr. Nasti,

whichever you prefer.

Although I have a feeling

you'll be adding daddy

to one of the variations

of my name by dawn.

Now then,

back to what I was saying

about trying to take you home tonight.

But before I do

there's a couple of things

I'd like to know

so that neither

of our time is wasted.

For starters,

I wanted to know

if sometime tonight

can I place my tongue

under the hood of your clit

and spell out the legacy

of my family tree

until you know the name

of my first relative

to be sold into slavery?

I mean,

if it's alright with you

that is.

Also,

because I have

a few fetishes

of my own,

I wanted to know

can I massage your feet

while kissing your legs

and sucking on your toes?

And when I get done

tending to your feet,

I was wondering

can I spread your cheeks

and eat your ass,

as well as your coochie,

like one would

a thanksgiving feast?

Cause I feel like

from looking at

the curvature of your body,

as well as the tone

and complexion of your skin,

that you'd make for

quite a delicious treat.

Now in my experience,

pleasure isn't just a one-way street.

And as much as I love to eat,

lord *knows* how much I do,

I happen to have this stiff dick

dangling not too far from my knees

that's throbbing to be inside

some part of you.

So if you don't mind,

I wanted to know

can I handcuff you

and test out

your ability to breathe through your nose

by resting my dick

balls deep in your throat?

While my dick is enveloped

in the warmth of your throat,

I'd be admiring how your eyes fill with tears

as you choke

from your mouth overflowing

with dick and spit

as you gag and jerk.

Mmmhhmmm, yeah

just thinking about it

got me wanting

to do that shit to you.

No need to worry though,

for your mouth

isn't the only hole

that I'm trying to fill.

Cause if it's cool with you

I was wondering

can I slide my dick in between your lower lips

and apply all of it

so that I'm stroking in and out

of your cervix

while occasionally hitting your uterus?

If that sounds like too much for you

just let me know.

There is another option

that I'd like to share with you

if I may be so bold.

I wanted to know

can I place you in my sex swing

and fuck you in your ass

till I stretch you out

to the point that you wouldn't be able

to make any noises

when you pass gas for a while?

And don't worry

I have a variety

of lubricants

in case

you think

that it would be

too painful

for you to do.

What's wrong?!?

You look a little startled

from everything I've said.

In fairness,

my last name is Nasti.

I hope you didn't think

that I was going to be asking

can I take you out sometime

or something along those lines.

I'm not sure if you've noticed,

but this whole time

that I been talking to you

I never once asked

can I know your name?

So,

about all the questions

that I *have* been asking you tonight.

I'm curious about if I

can I do those things to you

or not?

Regretfully reminiscing

We don't talk like we use to

and when we're around each other

things don't feel quite like they used to.

If I had to guess,

I'd say it's probably because of

my lack of drive

which has caused you

to shift to neutral.

A shift that has

resulted in you sliding back,

no longer heading in the direction

I was hoping for

us to be going.

Now I'm stuck here

feeling dumb as fuck

for allowing the possibility

of us being more than

just friends

to go by.

I can't help but

reminisce on what I missed out on

with you

because I was

 trying to test my luck

with opportunists

whose availability became non-existent

once my handouts

and willingness to do for them

and give to them

ran out.

Truth is,

I want to tell you how much I miss you.

From our never ending convos

about a slew of random things.

To our more stimulating private moments

that still bring a smile to my face,

as well as causing other physical reactions

to arise from me.

For though I only experienced a fraction of you,

my whole being still craves you.

I'm not sure if this is a goodbye letter,

or my way of

crying out to you

in the hope that you'll give me another shot.

I guess you can just say

that I was having a moment

while deep in my feelings.

I just want you to know

that I regret the decisions I've made

that have resulted

in me being

without you.

Differences

I ask you questions

that require detailed answers,

yet you give me short ass responses

that fail to address my concerns.

You say I do too much.

Which is funny

seeing as to how

I feel as though

you don't do enough.

You seem

to only see me one way.

While I see you another.

Life is largely about perceptions.

I guess ours are just different

from one another.

Closure

You helped create me,

but you didn't raise me.

You knew of me,

but you never really knew me.

I've heard a lot about you

by so many, but you.

The reason for your absence

still bothers me to this day.

But as I have grown and progressed in life,

so has my understanding of why things are the way they are.

And so, as I write this in memoriam to you,

I do not feel anger or resentment for the abuse and neglect I
experienced.

But rather I feel a weight lifted

and much relief gained.

As I feel I can finally have closure with you,

my father, though you have long since laid out to your eternal rest.

So as you sleep now forever more,

just know that your youngest child loves you

and wishes you the best.

Insanity

All I would like

is for you to be happy.

But as of late

you seem so sad and stressed.

I think it's because

you're with him,

cause you weren't like this before,

Ever since you've been with him,

all he's done

is make you cry in the morning

and leave you alone at night.

So that you're left

not only crying and alone,

but worrying about him

as well.

You confide in me

about the problems

between the two of you.

Partially because

I'm your best friend,

but also because

your family won't have

anything to do with you

since you refuse to

leave this unhealthy

and abusive

relationship you're in.

I always tell you

that you deserve better

and that you

would be better off

leaving him.

Which always leads to us arguing

and you telling me that you love him.

And how it isn't really that bad,

and you know he loves you

so one day he'll change.

Three months later

and you're telling me

about how things

are still the same

which to you

is a good thing.

Except I know that's not true.

I can tell by the weight you've lost,

the hair that's fallen out,

the occasional bruises I see on you.

Plus, now apparently your boyfriend

has another close female friend.

This time her name is Jessica,

probably the same chick

he was spending all day with

on your birthday.

As always,

You come to me

pleading for advice about what to do.

And as always,

I tell you that you should leave him

and find someone else

or just take time to yourself.

Because you deserve better

and shouldn't have to be put through

everything that you're going through.

You tell me that it isn't that easy

and that you can't leave him

because you love him

and he makes you feel like you matter.

I'm at a loss for words

and a loss for what to do

because it seems like

nothing I say

seems to matter to you.

Another two months' pass

and now he's practically ignoring

you completely,

except when he wants some money

or sex from you.

I'm just happy

that it looks like he's eased up

on beating you.

Though it's probably cause

I threatened to report him

after you had your

second miscarriage.

I've noticed that you've

turned a blind eye

to the hickeys left on him

and you don't even

say anything when he doesn't

come home for days on end.

I frequently tell you that you deserve better

and that at some point

enough has to be enough.

Again, you tell me that

I don't understand.

And that once he realizes

how much you love him

he'll change.

It's been about three weeks

since I've heard from you.

Your job said that

they haven't seen you

in about a week or so.

So I go to your house

to see what's up.

I knock, bang,

and call out your name

but no answer.

And even though I don't want to

I use the spare key you gave me to come in.

Soon as I enter your house,

a horrible smell hits me.

I call out for you

but get no answer.

I walk into your bedroom

and notice that your bathroom door is cracked open

with the light on.

I open it to find you slumped over

in the bathtub.

Your skin is pale

and appears to be riddled

with sores from you rotting away.

I count at least seven empty pill bottles

scattered across the floor.

But it's hard to tell

because my eyes are so blurry

from tears that I can't keep

from falling down my face.

As my tears slow and I'm able to look at you,

I can see that your eyes are open

and seem to be staring out

into nothing.

I can see that

your face is stained

with dried mascara,

likely from you crying.

On the window sill next to you

I see that there's a letter.

I open it

and immediately want to cry

once I start to read it

because it's addressed to me

like you knew

I would be the one to find you.

The letter says,

"I have, and always will, love him.

And now that I'm gone

he'll realize how much he loves me

and then he'll change".

As I stood there

holding the note, you wrote.

I break down

and tears began to fall

endlessly from my eyes.

For I felt responsible

for what happened to you.

Because it was I

who kept doing

and saying the same thing,

all the while

expecting different results

from you.

When deep down

a part of me knew

that you wouldn't change.

Now as I stand here,

looking at your lifeless

decayed body,

I can't help but think

how much better

you really deserved.

Gone, not forgotten

You were my heart.

The one who helped

lay the foundation

for who I am today.

During the times

when everything

seemed miserably dark,

and I felt constantly alone

and like no one understood me.

You were

the one who brightened my days

and made me unafraid to be myself.

You acknowledged me,

and showed me the kind of love

and appreciation I needed

in order to be a better person.

Your love

and support

served as my

warm blanket and pillow,

During a time,

when I was developing

and needed it most.

When life seemed to be

a repeating sad song

that made days longer

and harder to deal with.

Your presence changed the tune

to something that made life easier to deal with

and my days' pass by with ease.

The day you died,

the better part of me did as well.

And to this day,

it is a wound

which has never fully healed.

For quite some time,

my view of life

had become blurred

because of the constant tears

that I shed as a result

of losing you.

When I lost you,

I lost a mentor,

a friend,

and in so many ways,

a mother.

In this life

and in the next,

there will never be another

who will have such a great impact

on my life

as you did.

You are forever loved

and missed

by not only myself,

but the countless other lives

which you touched.

So know that

while you are gone now

and resting peacefully,

you are not,

nor will you ever be

forgotten.

A matter of Just us

One shot,

two shots,

where are the cops?

Three shots,

four shots,

when will it stop?

No, stop!

Please, stop!!

He can't breathe cop!!!

We riot

out of anger

and demand justice

for those wrongfully robbed

of their lives,

by those

who are supposed

to protect and serve.

But you tell us,

the victims

and the fearful,

to be quiet.

And that

more things matter than "just us".

And so

we scream,

"we matter!"

and "this must stop!".

But again,

you tell us to be silent.

Only this time

you tell through

your inaction

and the blinders

that you choose to wear

so that you don't have

to address the problem

we all see here.

But why must it be this way?

How come

you choose to allow us

to be treated this way?

Why do our issues

not matter to you

and those in your similar

position of power?

You acknowledge

that we matter

when we're providing you

with entertainment.

But we wish for

and demand for

more from

the ones who

once enslaved us.

And now take our fathers,

and give our mother's

limited resources to raise us.

So I say to you all now,

give us what is owed

and what we deserve,

or we will

burn down what we've built

and you take for granted

and then take

what should have

been given to us

to begin with.

Because this notion

that it is

just us

that can be

denied justice

is something

we are no longer

willing to tolerate.

What a place (Revised in 2016)

What a place,

oh what a place

we live in today.

A place considered to be

land of the free

and home of the brave.

But I ask you,

what is free

in this land that I reside in?

What is free

in this land that I run,

hide, and fight to survive in?

Living so,

because at any moment my life,

and the lives of so many others,

can easily be snuffed out

like candle lights

should we act a way

that people in power

wouldn't like.

Or even worse,

open our mouths

and say anything

that would offend them.

What a place

that the oppressed

have gotten to the point

that now

we as a people,

walk with our heads down

while holding down

each other,

far removed from the days

when we kept our heads held high,

supported one another,

and continuously marched forward.

Oh what a place

we live in today

where selling cigarette's, cd's,

and doing something as simple

as driving your vehicle

with your daughter in

the backseat

and significant other beside you

can lead to officers of the law

discharging their firearm

or strong arming you

to bringing your life

to an immediate halt.

Oh what a place

we live in today

where a simple traffic stop

for having your brake light out

can result in you being incarcerated

and ultimately your life ended,

and those responsible simply say

"wasn't our fault".

And the only justice brought about

for such injustices as these

is a social hashtag for the deceased

whose life was taken too soon.

Oh.

What

A.

Place.

Where those who are oppressed and treated unfairly

speak out about how their lives matter,

but are told not to worry or stress

because all lives matter.

Despite the fact that there is evidence

that shows that the lives of the oppressed

is held in less regard than all of the rest.

Oh what a place this is

where the pigment of your skin

plays a part in whether or not

you get a few months behind bars

or a life sentence

for the very same crime

that is committed.

Oh what a place we live in

where there are few left

who are brave enough to rightfully lead

and too many have long since forgotten

what it means to really be free.

What a place

oh what a place

this is indeed.

ill fated (Revised in 2016)

There was once a little boy

who lived happily with his family.

Until one day

the little boy told a secret

to someone who shouldn't have known.

A secret about how

the little boy was hurt

by a father who abused drugs

as well as his own son.

And a mother who would turn a blind eye

to the things done to the little boy

because the drugs which she used

she loved more than her own son

as well as

her other children that did not live in her home.

And so the little boy was taken from his family

as a result of the secret which he had told.

But it was not the little boy's fault

for he did not know

that he was not to be speaking to others

about the things that happen within his home.

Time has passed

and now the little boy is not so little.

He is often neglected by his loved ones

as well as bullied and mistreated

by many people that he meets.

He often acts out often

because anger is

his only outlet.

The only person who treated the boy

like he was someone worthwhile

died without notice,

leaving the boy with a wound

that would never heal right.

This wound would add

to the many others

that the boy harbored inside.

More time has now passed

and now the little boy is nearly a man.

He loves a girl who doesn't feel the same way for him.

It seems as though things are always this way for the boy.

Always being neglected, constantly dealing with heartache from loss,

and always troubled by the various forms of abuse

inflicted by not just his father and mother

but many others that the boy has not spoken of.

Which leaves the boy in a constant state of wondering,

"Is this God's plan for me?!?".

His nightly prayers for better days

have been replaced by silent tears

which he sheds nearly every night before he goes to sleep.

Each night much like the last,

with him hoping that when he wakes

it will all been just a dream.

Or better yet,

that he will not wake

and instead he will forever rest in peace.

For it is only in his sleep

that the scars and wounds from his experienced traumas

do not eat at him and continue to tear him apart.

At last,

more time has passed

and the once little boy is now a grown man.

Sadly, the pain that he has endured

from the things that he's experienced

throughout his life

has the boy prepared to end his life.

And so he writes

a goodbye letter to the few people that he knows

and brings the barrel of his gun

to the bridge of his nose.

His eyes fill with tears as he smiles

happily, because he can

feel the weight of his world lifted,

knowing that shortly

he will have no pain, stresses,

or worries anymore.

He pulls back on the trigger

and just like that

the once happy little boy

who became a damaged and broken man

is now no more.

Say what you wish

about the little boy and his final decision,

but be mindful that the little boy

did not ask for the life which he was given.

A prisoner to the choices of others,

and a victim to the traumas that haunted him constantly.

His life and death were both tragedies,

unfortunately, like so many others

the little boy was just born

ill fated.

Closing words

I would like to give a big thank you to everyone who has taken the time to delve into my mind and experience my art. What you've read is an accumulation of most of my poems over the span of my life up until now. I hope that you found my work to be enjoyable. When it comes to acknowledging those who played a part in inspiring me and pushing me to do my art, I feel I would need a whole other book in order to properly thank and acknowledge all of those individuals. With that said, I would like to whole heartedly thank all of my past and current friends, lovers, teachers, mentors, and fellow artist who have helped me along my journey of getting to where I am now. To my family, know that you all have played your respective parts in me getting to where I am now, and for that I am equally grateful and appreciative. Again, I am deeply indebted to and humbled by those who have supported me and my art, you will forever have my thanks. I look forward to the things that will come after this book, and I wish the best for whomever may be reading this as well.